CLASSIC RAGS

~

FOR

FLUTE

&

PIANO

MUSIC MINUS ONE

SUGGESTIONS FOR USING THIS MMO EDITION

WE HAVE TRIED to create a product that will provide you an easy way to learn and perform these ragtime classics with a complete accompaniment in the comfort of your own home. Because it involves a fixed accompaniment performance, there is an inherent lack of flexibility in tempo. The following MMO features and techniques will reduce these inflexibilities and help you maximize the effectiveness of the MMO practice and performance system:

We have observed generally accepted tempi, but some may wish to perform at a different tempo, or to slow down or speed up the accompaniment for practice purposes. You can purchase from MMO specialized CD players and recorders which allow variable speed while maintaining proper pitch. This is an indispensable tool for the serious musician and you may wish to look into purchasing this useful piece of equipment for full enjoyment of all your MMO editions.

Where the performer begins a piece *solo* or without an introduction from the accompanying instrument, we have provided a set of subtle taps before each piece as appropriate to help you enter with the proper tempo.

We want to provide you with the most useful practice and performance accompaniments possible. If you have any suggestions for improving the MMO system, please feel free to contact us. You can reach us by e-mail at *mmogroup@musicminusone.com*.

3372

CONTENTS

All selections arranged and edited by Anne and Jeff Barnhart

NOTES ON THE PIECES

RAGTIME WAS THE MOST POPULAR MUSIC IN AMERICA for about twenty years, from the late 1890s to 1917. This genre deftly combined classical structures and harmonies with a new level and variety of syncopation. The syncopated rhythms of ragtime set it apart from any previous music and present the performer with unique challenges.

The performance notes that follow will concern each of the nine rags presented in this collection individually. In general each rag is presented in its original form the first time through each section, with ornaments and variations introduced on the repeats. Younger or less-experienced players can enjoy these works by simply playing the easier ornament-free version through the repeat of any section with variations. Remember, in all ragtime pieces, the accents most often fall between the beats. This syncopation alone is the element that gives ragtime its vitality. Accent carefully!

Common ornamentation notation is used extensively in this edition. Examples of these notations are below.

ENJOY!

∽

THE ENTERTAINER (1902)

Familiar, fun and fantastic, *The Entertainer* is known and loved by all. This and all of the Joplin rags in this collection are examples of "classic" rags. Joplin's rags are classical in form, counterpoint and harmony. The brilliance of this work is enhanced by our variations, which take the repeats of the B and D sections up an octave into the highest range of the flute. Practice these sections slowly with much breath support and firm articulation. Remember, if these high notes are too challenging right now just repeat the original section. Section C features a call and response with the piano. Listen carefully and try to meld with it. On the repeat of C, the piano takes the lead, so play your countermelodies quietly and as accompaniment.

PINE APPLE RAG (1901)

Along with *The Entertainer* and *Solace*, *Pine Apple Rag* enjoyed a resurgence of popularity when it was featured in the 1973 motion picture, *The Sting*. This rag is highly syncopated even by ragtime's standards. The difficulty of the syncopation can be overcome if you remove any ties (and possibly slurs) from the melodies and practice them tonguing each note. This technique will allow you to hear the length of the pitch itself. Once your ear is accustomed to the sound, add the ties back for the true rhythm. Remember, as in all syncopation, the accents often come between the beats rather than on them. On the repeats of B and D, I have inserted double-tonguing in several sections of the melodies. Keep your tongue relaxed in order to better articulate the sections. Of course, you can always return to the first statement of a section if any variations prove too tricky.

SOLACE (1909)

This piece incorporates a Spanish rhythm. While it is written in 2/4, it is actually felt in 4/8, perhaps because of the languid tempo. Keep four beats in mind and you will find its rhythms unfold more smoothly for you. The challenge of *Solace* lies not in the melodic structure or even in the rhythm of the various sections but in tone, breath-control and pitch. You must take full, deep breaths, support your sound and listen to the piano for a tonal center. While we have kept the *rubato* to a minimum, you will hear flute and piano leaning into the music, especially on each presentation of the A section. On the repeat of A between B and C, flute and piano trade off on the melody in one-measure increments. Be sure that you keep your melodic statements connected to those in the piano: become one with the piano to create a seamless line. Finally, all *fermatas* you encounter in the piece are held for double the value of the written note.

Solace is one of Joplin's "Mozart" pieces, where the difficulty lies below the surface and a truly beautiful, musical presentation requires much diligence, effort and listening.

RAGTIME ORIOLE (1911)

When tackling this virtuosic piece, you must apply the trite but tried and true adage: slow and steady wins the race. This piece spans a melodic range of three octaves, with melodies that sweep by as do birds on the breeze. To execute these acrobatic maneuvers, concentrate on full, deep breaths. In section C, be aware of the key signature and especially of the double flats. Remember, "do 'em like you say 'em," meaning that you would say "B double flat" and not "B♭ double flat." Lowering your B two half-steps will give you A. Section D features double tonguing on the repeat. For an easier version simply omit it. If you do the double tongue, remember to keep your tongue loose and support it with sufficient air. Start slowly and in time your speed and accuracy will increase day by day until you achieve the desired speed

BLUE GOOSE (1916)

This is a light, happy piece with a contrasting, lyrical central section, which has the unusual distinction of possessing no syncopation. Special attention should be paid to articulation and accuracy in the A and B sections. Often, you can hear the piano playing a harmonic line that matches the rhythm of your melody The beautiful C section should be played with an expansive and well-supported tone. During the repeat of the C section, there is ample ornamentation. Strive to keep the ornaments flowing with the phrase and do not allow them to break the fluidity of the melodic line.

RAGTIME NIGHTENGALE (1915)

In this melancholic, stately rag, the flute once again mimics a bird. This time our bird is warbling a lovely nocturne. The most difficult aspect of this piece is its slurred intervals. The melodic line is destroyed if the intervals are not executed with smoothness and with tonal beauty intact. Initially, practice this piece by tonguing all of the intervals. When you are ready, insert the slurs. If the repeat of section C is too challenging, play the simple statement of the melody found in the first time through C twice.

GLADIOLUS RAG (1907)

Gladiolus presents its challenges by way of key signature. We begin in A♭ and move to D♭ in the C and D sections. Before tackling this piece, review and perfect your A♭ and D♭ scales. Passing be the traditional scalar boundaries, practice these scales from your low C up to C4. Also, review your trill fingerings for the repeat of section D, keeping the key signature in mind.

ECHO OF SPRING (1935)

This rag is the only piece in the collection that is through-composed. Unlike most other pieces in the ragtime genre, it is void of key changes and separation by section or repeats. It was written by Stride pianist Willie "the Lion" Smith, and as such it is also the most jazz-based rag. As with *Solace*, pitch, breath-support and tone are paramount. Play the sixteenth-note triplets carefully, making sure that they land on the beat and not before. Articulation should be smooth and *legato* throughout. The trick is to make this difficult piece sound lazy and relaxed.

THE BIRDS' CARNIVAL (1935)

The Birds' Carnival is an example of a novelty rag. Composers of these rags were usually more classically trained, an attribute that shows up in their advanced harmonies and intricate melodies. As with *Ragtime Oriole*, the flute represents our feathered friends in this piece. Play with a light (not thin), buoyant sound.

Rhythmically, this rag is more challenging because it is written in Common Time, but is played in Cut Time. Practice it slowly in 4/4, gradually adding speed until it slides comfortably into 2/4. The repeat of section B is done in a canon, with the piano leading. The C section changes radically from G to E♭, so watch your key change. Section C features rapid arpeggios on the repeat. Practice these outside the context of the piece until they flow. A good technique is to practice the arpeggios down and up and then in reverse.

—Anne Barnhart

The Entertainer
A Rag Time Two Step

Pine Apple Rag

Scott Joplin
(1868-1917)

MMO 3372

Solace
A Mexican Serenade

Scott Joplin
(1868-1917)

Ragtime Oriole

James Scott
(1885-1938)

Two measures of taps precede music.

Do not play this piece fast.

98

103

108

113

116

D.S. al Fine

Blue Goose
Rag

Charles L. Johnson
(1876-1950)
as Raymond Birch

Ragtime Nightengale

Joseph Lamb
(1887-1960)

Gladiolus Rag

Scott Joplin
(1868-1917)

MMO 3372

Echo of Spring

Willie "the Lion" Smith
(1897-1973)
Clarence Williams
(1898-1965)
Tausha Hammed

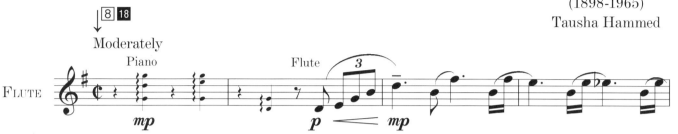

MMO 3372

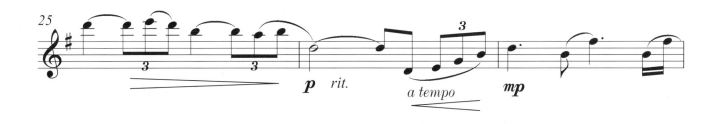

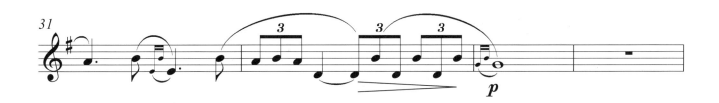

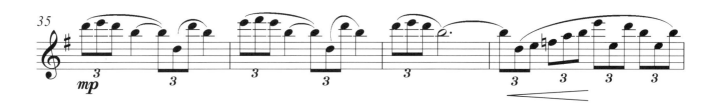

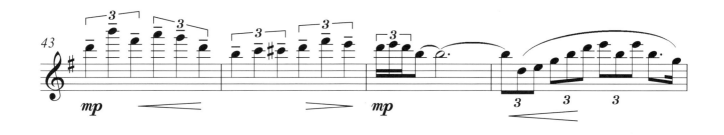

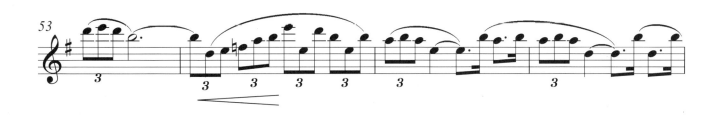

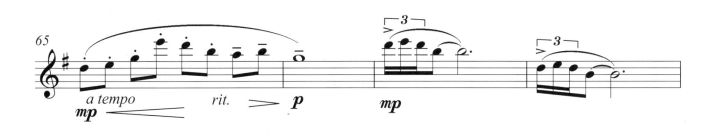

The Birds' Carnival

Edward 'Zez' Confrey
(1895-1971)

Two measures of taps precede music.

Allegretto grazioso

Flute

MUSIC MINUS ONE
50 Executive Boulevard
Elmsford, New York 10523-1325
1.800.669.7464 U.S. ← 914.592.1188 International

www.musicminusone.com
mmogroup@musicminusone.com